Contents

The Moon *Robert Louis Stevenson* 6
The Land of Counterpane
   Robert Louis Stevenson 7
Limericks *Edward Lear* 8
The Duel *Eugene Field* 10
The Owl and the Pussycat *Edward Lear* 12
The Sugarplum Tree *Eugene Field* 14
A Swing Song *William Allingham* 16
The Months *Sara Coleridge* 18
Turtle Soup *Lewis Carroll* 22
Winter *Alfred, Lord Tennyson* 23
The Cats Have Come to Tea
   Kate Greenaway 24
The Wind *Robert Louis Stevenson* 25
The North Wind Doth Blow *Anonymous* 26
The Lamb *William Blake* 28
Laughing Song *William Blake* 28
The City Mouse and the Garden Mouse
Christina Rossetti 29
Pied Beauty *Gerard Manley Hopkins* 30
Ducks' Ditty *Kenneth Grahame* 31
Foreign Lands *Robert Louis Stevenson* ... 32
The Land of Story-books
   Robert Louis Stevenson 33
A Nonsense Alphabet *Edward Lear* 34
Jabberwocky *Lewis Carroll* 40
The Crocodile *Lewis Carroll* 41
Wynken, Blynken, and Nod *Eugene Field* ... 42
To a Butterfly *William Wordsworth* 44
Sweet Peas *John Keats* 45
The Violet *William Wordsworth* 45
Hiawatha's Childhood
   Henry Wadsworth Longfellow 46
The Eagle *Alfred, Lord Tennyson* 48
White Butterflies
   Algernon Charles Swinburne 48
The Witches' Spell *William Shakespeare* ... 49
The Twelve Days of Christmas
   Anonymous 50

The Night Before Christmas
   Clement C. Moore 50
Queen Mab *Thomas Hood* 53
The Pobble Who Has No Toes
   Edward Lear 54
Rain *Robert Louis Stevenson* 56
Horses of the Sea *Christina Rossetti* 56
Time to Rise *Robert Louis Stevenson* 57
Who Has Seen the Wind?
   Christina Rossetti 57
Merry Autumn Days *Charles Dickens* 58
The Kitten and the Falling Leaves
   William Wordsworth 59
A Song About Myself *John Keats* 60
Travelling *Anonymous* 61
Winter *William Shakespeare* 62
Windy Nights *Robert Louis Stevenson* ... 62
December *Robert Southey* 63
My Shadow *Robert Louis Stevenson* 64
What is Pink? *Christina Rossetti* 65
The Daffodils *William Wordsworth* 66
Pippa's Song *Robert Browning* 67
Upon the Snail *John Bunyan* 67
The Village Blacksmith
   Henry Wadsworth Longfellow 68
Trees *Sara Coleridge* 69
When the Cows Come Home
   Christina Rossetti 69
Old Meg *John Keats* 70
The Lady of Shalott
   Alfred, Lord Tennyson 72
Minnie and Winnie
   Alfred, Lord Tennyson 74
The Owl *Alfred, Lord Tennyson* 75
The Mountain and the Squirrel
   Ralph Waldo Emerson 76
Be Like the Bird *Victor Hugo* 77
The Fairies *William Allingham* 77

Copyright © MCMLXXXVIII by Cliveden Press.
All rights reserved.
Published by Cliveden Press,
An Egmont Company, Egmont House,
P.O. Box 111, Great Ducie Street,
Manchester M60 3BL.
Printed in Hungary.
ISBN 7235 1615 4

TRADITIONAL CHILDREN'S VERSE

illustrated by
EILEEN FITZPATRICK BERRY

CLIVEDEN PRESS

THE MOON

The moon has a face like the clock in the hall;
She shines on thieves on the garden wall,
On streets and fields and harbour quays,
And birdies asleep in the forks of the trees.

The squalling cat and the squeaking mouse,
The howling dog by the door of the house,
The bat that lies in bed at noon,
All love to be out by the light of the moon.

But all of the things that belong to the day
Cuddle to sleep to be out of her way;
And flowers and children close their eyes
Till up in the morning the sun shall arise.

Robert Louis Stevenson

THE LAND OF COUNTERPANE

When I was sick and lay a-bed,
I had two pillows at my head,
And all my toys beside me lay
To keep me happy all the day.

And sometimes for an hour or so
I watched my leaden soldiers go,
With different uniforms and drills,
Among the bedclothes, through the hills;

And sometimes sent my ships in fleets
All up and down among the sheets;
Or brought my trees and houses out,
And planted cities all about.

I was the giant great and still
That sits upon the pillow-hill,
And see before him dale and plain,
The pleasant land of counterpane.

Robert Louis Stevenson

LIMERICKS

There was an Old Man with a beard,
Who said, "It is just as I feared!
Two Owls and a Hen,
Four Larks and a Wren
Have all built their nests in my beard!"

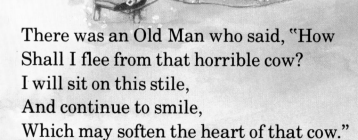

There was an Old Man who said, "How
Shall I flee from that horrible cow?
I will sit on this stile,
And continue to smile,
Which may soften the heart of that cow."

There was an Old Man in a tree,
Who was horribly bored by a bee.
When they said, "Does it buzz?"
He replied, "Yes, it does!
It's a regular brute of a bee!"

There was an Old Man with a nose,
Who said, "If you choose to suppose
That my nose is too long, you are certainly wrong!"
That remarkable Man with a nose.

There was a Young Lady of Welling,
Whose praise all the world was a-telling;
She played on the harp, and caught several Carp,
That accomplished Young Lady of Welling.

Edward Lear

THE DUEL

The gingham dog and the calico cat
Side by side on the table sat;
   'Twas half-past twelve, and (what do you think!)
   Nor one nor t' other had slept a wink!
   The old Dutch clock and the Chinese plate
   Appeared to know as sure as fate
There was going to be a terrible spat.
   (I wasn't there; I simply state
   What was told to me by the Chinese plate!)

The gingham dog went, "bow-wow-wow!"
And the calico cat replied, "mee-ow!"
   The air was littered, an hour or so,
   With bits of gingham and calico,
   While the old Dutch clock in the chimney-place
   Up with its hands before it face,
For it always dreaded a family row.
   (Now mind: I'm only telling you
   What the old Dutch clock declares is true!)

The Chinese plate looked very blue,
And wailed, "Oh, dear! what shall we do!"
  But the gingham dog and the calico cat
  Wallowed this way and tumbled that,
  Employing every tooth and claw
  In the awfullest way you ever saw—
And, oh! how the gingham and calico flew!
  (Don't fancy I exaggerate—
  I got my news from the Chinese plate!)

Next morning, where the two had sat
They found no trace of dog or cat;
  And some folks think unto this day
  That burglars stole that pair away!
  But the truth about the cat and pup
  Is this: they ate each other up!
Now what do you really think of that!
  (The old Dutch clock it told me so,
  And that is how I came to know.)

Eugene Field

11

THE OWL AND THE PUSSYCAT

The Owl and the Pussycat went to sea
In a beautiful pea-green boat;
They took some honey, and plenty of money
Wrapped up in a five-pound note.
The Owl looked up to the stars above,
And sang to a small guitar,
"O lovely Pussy, O Pussy, my love,
What a beautiful Pussy you are,
You are,
You are!
What a beautiful Pussy you are!"

Pussy said to the Owl, "You elegant fowl,
How charmingly sweet you sing!
Oh! let us be married; too long we have tarried:
But what shall we do for a ring?"
They sailed away, for a year and a day,
To the land where the bong-tree grows,
And there in a wood a Piggy-wig stood,
With a ring at the end of his nose,
His nose,
His nose,
With a ring at the end of his nose.

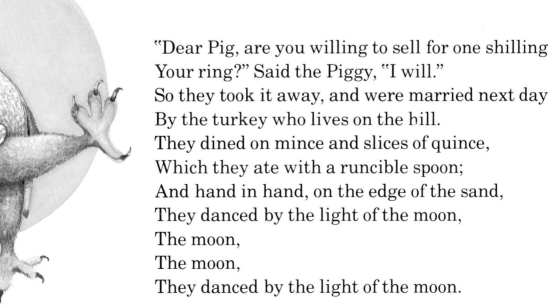

"Dear Pig, are you willing to sell for one shilling
Your ring?" Said the Piggy, "I will."
So they took it away, and were married next day
By the turkey who lives on the hill.
They dined on mince and slices of quince,
Which they ate with a runcible spoon;
And hand in hand, on the edge of the sand,
They danced by the light of the moon,
The moon,
The moon,
They danced by the light of the moon.

Edward Lear

THE SUGARPLUM TREE

Have you ever heard of the Sugarplum Tree?
'Tis a marvel of great renown!
It blooms on the shore of the Lollipop Sea
In the garden of Shut-eye Town;
The fruit that it bears is so wondrously sweet
(As those who have tasted it say)
That good little children have only to eat
Of that fruit to be happy next day.

When you've got to the tree, you would have a hard time
To capture the fruit which I sing;
The tree is so tall that no person could climb
To the boughs where the sugarplums swing!
But up in that tree sits a chocolate cat,
And a gingerbread dog prowls below —
And this is the way you contrive to get at
Those sugarplums tempting you so:

You say but the word to that gingerbread dog
And he barks with such terrible zest
That the chocolate cat is at once all agog,
As her swelling proportions attest.
And the chocolate cat goes cavorting around
From this leafy limb unto that,
And the sugarplums tumble, of course, to the ground —
Hurrah for that chocolate cat!

There are marshmallows, gumdrops, and peppermint canes,
With stripings of scarlet or gold,
And you carry away of the treasure that rains
As much as your apron can hold!
So come, little child, cuddle close to me
In your dainty white nightcap and gown,
And I'll rock you away to that Sugarplum Tree
In the garden of Shut-eye Town.

Eugene Field

15

A SWING SONG

Swing, swing,
Sing, sing,
Here! my throne and I am a king!
Swing, sing,
Swing, sing,
Farewell, earth, for I'm on the wing!

Low, high,
Here I fly,
Like a bird through sunny sky;
Free, free,
Over the lea,
Over the mountain, over the sea!

Up, down,
Up and down,
Which is the way to London Town?
Where? Where?
Up in the air,
Close your eyes and now you are there!

Soon, soon,
Afternoon,
Over the sunset, over the moon;
Far, far,
Over all bar,
Sweeping on from star to star!

No, no,
Low, low,
Sweeping daisies with my toe.
Slow, slow,
To and fro,
Slow – slow – slow – slow.

William Allingham

THE MONTHS

January brings the snow,
Makes our feet and fingers glow.

February brings the rain,
Thaws the frozen lake again.

March brings breezes loud and shrill,
Stirs the dancing daffodil.

April brings the primrose sweet,
Scatters daisies at our feet.

May brings flocks of pretty lambs,
Skipping by their fleecy dams.

June brings tulips, lilies, roses,
Fills the children's hands with posies.

Hot July brings cooling showers,
Apricots and gillyflowers.

August brings the sheaves of corn;
Then the harvest home is borne.

Warm September brings the fruit;
Sportsmen then begin to shoot.

Fresh October brings the pheasant;
Then to gather nuts is pleasant.

Dull November brings the blast,
When the leaves are whirling fast.

Chill December brings the sleet,
Blazing fires and Christmas treat.

Sara Coleridge

TURTLE SOUP

Beautiful Soup, so rich and green,
Waiting in a hot tureen!
Who for such dainties would not stoop?
Soup of the evening, beautiful Soup!
Soup of the evening, beautiful Soup!
Beau—ootiful Soo—oop!
Beau—ootiful Soo—oop!
Soo—oop of the e—e—evening,
Beautiful, beautiful Soup!

Beautiful Soup! Who cares for fish,
Game, or any other dish?
Who would not give all else for two
Pennyworth only of beautiful Soup?
Pennyworth only of beautiful Soup?
Beau—ootiful Soo—oop!
Beau—ootiful Soo—oop!
Soo—oop of the e—e—evening,
Beautiful, beauti—FUL SOUP!

Lewis Carroll

WINTER

The frost is here,
The fuel is dear,
And woods are sear,
And fires burn clear,
And frost is here,
And has bitten the heel of the going year.

Bite, frost, bite!
You roll up away from the light,
The blue wood-louse and the plump dormouse,
And the bees are stilled and the flies are killed,
And you bite far into the heart of the house,
But not into mine.

Bite, frost, bite!
The woods are all the searer,
The fuel is all the dearer,
The fires are all the clearer,
My spring is all the nearer,
You have bitten into the heart of the earth,
But not into mine.

Alfred, Lord Tennyson

THE CATS HAVE COME TO TEA

What did she see—oh, what did she see,
As she stood leaning against the tree?
Why, all the cats had come to tea.

What a fine turn-out from round about!
All the houses had let them out,
And here they were with scamper and shout.

"Mew, mew, mew!" was all they could say,
And, "We hope we find you well today."

Oh, what would she do—oh, what should she do?
What a lot of milk they would get through;
For here they were with, "Mew, mew, mew!"

She did not know—oh, she did not know,
If bread and butter they'd like or no;
They might want little mice, oh! oh! oh!

Dear me—oh, dear me,
All the cats had come to tea.

Kate Greenaway

THE WIND

I saw you toss the kites on high
And blow the birds about the sky;
And all around I heard you pass,
Like ladies' skirts across the grass—
  O wind, a-blowing all day long,
  O wind, that sings so loud a song!

I saw the different things you did,
But always you yourself you hid.
I felt you push, I heard you call,
I could not see yourself at all—
  O wind, a-blowing all day long,
  O wind, that sings so loud a song!

O you that are so strong and cold,
O blower, are you young or old?
Are you a beast of field and tree,
Or just a stronger child than me?
  O wind, a-blowing all day long,
  O wind, that sings so loud a song!

Robert Louis Stevenson

25

THE NORTH WIND DOTH BLOW

The north wind doth blow,
And we shall have snow,
And what will the robin do then, Poor thing?
He'll sit in a barn,
And keep himself warm,
And hide his head under his wing, Poor thing!

The north wind doth blow,
And we shall have snow,
And what will the swallow do then, Poor thing?
Oh, do you not know
That he's off long ago,
To a country where he will find spring, Poor thing!

The north wind doth blow,
And we shall have snow,
And what will the dormouse do then, Poor thing?
Roll'd up like a ball,
In his nest snug and small,
He'll sleep till warm weather comes in, Poor thing!

The north wind doth blow,
And we shall have snow,
And what will the honey-bee do then, Poor thing?
In his hive he will stay
Till the cold is away,
And then he'll come out in the spring, Poor thing!

The north wind doth blow,
And we shall have snow,
And what will the children do then, Poor things?
When lessons are done,
They must skip, jump, and run,
Until they have made themselves warm, Poor things!

Anonymous

THE LAMB

Little lamb, who made thee?
Dost thou know who made thee?
Gave thee life and bid thee feed
By the stream and o'er the mead;
Gave thee clothing of delight,
Softest clothing, woolly, bright;
Gave thee such a tender voice,
Making all the vales rejoice;
    Little lamb, who made thee?
    Dost thou know who made thee?

Little lamb, I'll tell thee,
Little lamb, I'll tell thee.
He is called by thy name,
For He calls Himself a Lamb;
He is meek and He is mild,
He became a little child.
I a child, and thou a lamb,
We are called by His name.
    Little lamb, God bless thee,
    Little lamb, God bless thee.

William Blake

LAUGHING SONG

When the green woods laugh
  with the voice of joy,
And the dimpling stream
  runs laughing by,
When the air does laugh
  with our merry wit,
And the green hill laughs
  with the noise of it;
When the meadows laugh
  with lively green,
And the grasshopper laughs
  in the merry scene,

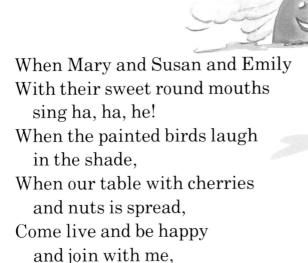

When Mary and Susan and Emily
With their sweet round mouths
   sing ha, ha, he!
When the painted birds laugh
   in the shade,
When our table with cherries
   and nuts is spread,
Come live and be happy
   and join with me,
To sing the sweet chorus
   of ha, ha, he!

William Blake

THE CITY MOUSE
AND THE
GARDEN MOUSE

The city mouse lives in a house;
The garden mouse lives in a bower.
He's friendly with the frogs and toads,
And sees the pretty plants in flower.

The city mouse eats bread and cheese;
The garden mouse eats what he can.
We will not grudge him seeds and stocks,
Poor little timid furry man.

Christina Rossetti

PIED BEAUTY

Glory be to God for dappled things –
For skies of couple-colour as a brinded cow;
For rose-moles all in stipple upon trout that swim;
Fresh-firecoal chestnut-falls; finches' wings;
Landscape plotted and pieced – fold, fallow, and plough;
And all trades, their gear and tackle and trim.

All things counter, original, spare, strange;
Whatever is fickle, freckled (who knows how?)
With swift, slow; sweet, sour; adazzle, dim;
He fathers-forth whose beauty is past change:
Praise Him.

Gerard Manley Hopkins

30

DUCKS' DITTY

All along the backwater,
Through the rushes tall,
Ducks are a-dabbling,
Up tails all!

Ducks' tails, drakes' tails,
Yellow feet a-quiver,
Yellow bills all out of sight
Busy in the river!

Slushy green undergrowth
Where the roach swim –
Here we keep our larder,
Cool and full and dim.

Everyone for what he likes!
We like to be
Heads down, tails up,
Dabbling free!

High in the blue above
Swifts whirl and call –
We are down a-dabbling,
Up tails all!

Kenneth Grahame

FOREIGN LANDS

Up into the cherry tree
Who should climb but little me?
I held the trunk with both my hands
And looked abroad on foreign lands.

I saw the next door garden lie,
Adorned with flowers, before my eye,
And many pleasant places more
That I had never seen before.

I saw the dimpling river pass
And be the sky's blue looking-glass;
The dusty roads go up and down
With people tramping in to town.

If I could find a higher tree
Farther and farther I should see,
To where the grown-up river slips
Into the sea among the ships.

To where the roads on either hand
Lean onward into fairy land,
Where all the children dine at five,
And all the playthings come alive.

Robert Louis Stevenson

THE LAND OF STORY-BOOKS

At evening when the lamp is lit,
Around the fire my parents sit;
They sit at home and talk and sing,
And do not play at anything.

Now, with my little gun, I crawl
All in the dark along the wall,
And follow round the forest track
Away behind the sofa back.

There, in the night, where none can spy,
All in my hunter's camp I lie,
And play at books that I have read
Till it is time to go to bed.

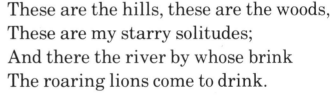

These are the hills, these are the woods,
These are my starry solitudes;
And there the river by whose brink
The roaring lions come to drink.

I see the others far away
As if in firelit camp they lay,
And I, like to an Indian scout,
Around their party prowled about.

So, when my nurse comes in for me,
Home I return across the sea,
And go to bed with backward looks
At my dear land of story-books.

Robert Louis Stevenson

A NONSENSE ALPHABET

A   was an ape,
Who stole some white tape
And tied up his toes
In four beautiful bows.
   a!
Funny old Ape!

B   was a bat,
Who slept all the day
And fluttered about
When the sun went away.
   b!
Brown little Bat!

C   was a camel,
You rode on his hump
And if you fell off,
You came down such a bump!
   c!
What a high Camel!

D   was a dove
Who lived in a wood
With such pretty soft wings,
And so gentle and good.
   d!
Dear little Dove!

E   was an eagle
Who sat on the rocks
And looked down on the fields
And the far away flocks.
   e!
Beautiful Eagle!

F   was a fan
Made of beautiful stuff
And when it was used
It went – Puffy-puff-puff!
   f!
Nice little Fan!

G   was a gooseberry
Perfectly red;
To be made into jam
And eaten with bread.
   g!
Gooseberry red!

H   was a heron
Who stood in a stream
The length of his neck
And his legs, was extreme.
   h!
Long-legged Heron!

I was an inkstand
Which stood on a table
With a nice pen to write with,
When we were able!
　i!
Neat little Inkstand!

J was a jug,
So pretty and white
With fresh water in it
At morning and night.
　j!
Nice little Jug!

K was a kingfisher,
Quickly he flew
So bright and so pretty,
Green, purple and blue.
　k!
Kingfisher, blue!

L was a lily
So white and so sweet
To see it and smell it
Was quite a nice treat!
　l!
Beautiful Lily!

M　was a man,
Who walked round and round,
And he wore a long coat
That came down to the ground.
　　m!
Funny old Man!

N　was a nut
So smooth and so brown,
And when it was ripe
It fell tumble-dum-down.
　　n!
Nice little Nut!

O　was an oyster
Who lived in his shell,
If you left him alone
He felt perfectly well.
　　o!
Open-mouthed Oyster!

P　was a polly
All red, blue and green
The most beautiful polly
That ever was seen.
　　p!
Poor little Polly!

Q　was a quill
Made into a pen,
But I do not know where
And I cannot say when.
　　q!
Nice little Quill!

R　was a rattlesnake
Rolled up so tight,
Those who saw him ran quickly
For fear he should bite.

　r!
Rattlesnake bite!

S　was a screw
To screw down a box
And then it was fastened
Without any locks.

　s!
Valuable Screw!

T　was a thimble
Of silver so bright
When placed on the finger
It fitted so tight!

　t!
Nice little Thimble!

U　was an upper-coat
Woolly and warm
To wear over all
In the snow or the storm.

　u!
What a nice Upper-coat!

V   was a veil
With a border upon it
And a riband to tie it
All round a pink bonnet.
   v!
Pretty green Veil!

W   was a watch
Where in letters of gold
The hour of the day
You might always behold.
   w!
Beautiful Watch!

X   was King Xerxes
Who wore on his head
A mighty large turban,
Green, yellow and red.
   x!
Look at King Xerxes!

Y   was a yak
From the land of Tibet
Except his white tail
He was all black as jet.
   y!
Look at the Yak!

Z   was a zebra,
All striped white and black,
And if he were tame
You might ride on his back.
   z!
Pretty striped Zebra!

Edward Lear

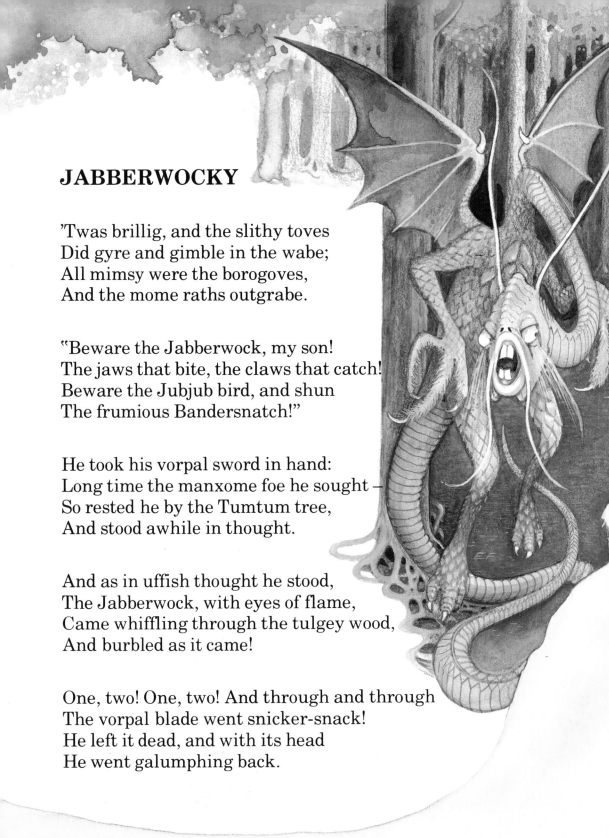

JABBERWOCKY

'Twas brillig, and the slithy toves
Did gyre and gimble in the wabe;
All mimsy were the borogoves,
And the mome raths outgrabe.

"Beware the Jabberwock, my son!
The jaws that bite, the claws that catch!
Beware the Jubjub bird, and shun
The frumious Bandersnatch!"

He took his vorpal sword in hand:
Long time the manxome foe he sought –
So rested he by the Tumtum tree,
And stood awhile in thought.

And as in uffish thought he stood,
The Jabberwock, with eyes of flame,
Came whiffling through the tulgey wood,
And burbled as it came!

One, two! One, two! And through and through
The vorpal blade went snicker-snack!
He left it dead, and with its head
He went galumphing back.

"And hast thou slain the Jabberwock?
Come to my arms, my beamish boy!
O frabjous day! Callooh! Callay!"
He chortled in his joy.

'Twas brillig, and the slithy toves
Did gyre and gimble in the wabe;
All mimsy were the borogoves,
And the mome raths outgrabe.

Lewis Carroll

THE CROCODILE

How doth the little crocodile
Improve his shining tail,
And pour the waters of the Nile
On every golden scale!

How cheerfully he seems to grin,
How neatly spreads his claws,
And welcomes little fishes in,
With gently smiling jaws!

Lewis Carroll

WYNKEN, BLYNKEN, AND NOD

Wynken, Blynken, and Nod one night
  sailed off in a wooden shoe—
Sailed on a river of crystal light
  into a sea of dew.
"Where are you going, and what do you wish?"
  the old moon asked the three.
"We have come to fish for the herring-fish
  that live in this beautiful sea;
Nets of silver and gold have we,"
    said Wynken,
    Blynken,
    and Nod.

The old moon laughed and sang a song,
  as they rocked in the wooden shoe;
And the wind that sped them all night long
  ruffled the waves of dew.
The little stars were the herring-fish
  that lived in the beautiful sea.
"Now cast your nets wherever you wish—
  never afraid are we!"
So cried the stars to the fishermen three,
    Wynken,
    Blynken,
    and Nod.

All night long their nets they threw
   to the stars in the twinkling foam—
Then down from the skies came the wooden shoe,
   bringing the fishermen home:
'Twas all so pretty a sail, it seemed
   as if it could not be,
And some folk thought 'twas a dream they'd dreamed
   of sailing that beautiful sea;
But I shall name you the fishermen three:
     Wynken,
     Blynken,
     and Nod.

Wynken and Blynken are two little eyes,
   and Nod is a little head,
And the wooden shoe that sailed the skies
   is a wee one's trundle bed.
So shut your eyes while Mother sings
   of wonderful sights that be,
And you shall see the beautiful things
   as you rock in the misty sea
Where the old shoe rocked the fishermen three,
     Wynken,
     Blynken,
     and Nod.

Eugene Field

TO A BUTTERFLY

I've watched you now a full half-hour,
Self-poised upon that yellow flower;
And, little Butterfly! indeed
I know not if you sleep or feed.
How motionless! – not frozen seas
More motionless! And then
What joy awaits you, when the breeze
Hath found you out among the trees,
And calls you forth again!

This plot of orchard-ground is ours;
My trees they are, my Sister's flowers.
Here rest your wings when they are weary;
Here lodge as in a sanctuary!
Come often to us, fear no wrong;
Sit near us on the bough!
We'll talk of sunshine and of song,
And summer days, when we were young;
Sweet childish days, that were as long
As twenty days are now.

William Wordsworth

SWEET PEAS

Here are sweet peas, on tiptoe for a flight,
With wings of gentle flush o'er delicate white,
And taper fingers catching at all things,
To bind them all about with tiny rings.

John Keats

THE VIOLET

A violet by a mossy stone,
Half hidden from the eye,
Fair as a star, when only one
Is shining in the sky.

William Wordsworth

HIAWATHA'S CHILDHOOD

By the shores of Gitche Gumee,
By the shining Big-Sea-Water,
Stood the wigwam of Nokomis,
Daughter of the Moon, Nokomis.
Dark behind it rose the forest,
Rose the black and gloomy pine-trees,
Rose the firs with cones upon them;
Bright before it beat the water,
Beat the clear and sunny water,
Beat the shining Big-Sea-Water.

At the door on summer evenings
Sat the little Hiawatha;
Heard the whispering of the pine-trees,
Heard the lapping of the waters,
Sounds of music, words of wonder;
"Minne-wawa!" said the pine-trees,
"Mudway-aushka!" said the water.
Saw the firefly, Wah-wah-taysee,
Flitting through the dusk of evening,
With the twinkle of its candle
Lighting up the brakes and bushes,
And he sang the song of children,
Sang the song Nokomis taught him:
"Wah-wah-taysee, little firefly,
Little, flitting, white-fire insect,
Little, dancing, white-fire creature,
Light me with your little candle,
Ere upon my bed I lay me,
Ere in sleep I close my eyelids!"

Then the little Hiawatha
Learned of every bird its language,
Learned their names and all their secrets,
How they built their nest in Summer,
Where they hid themselves in Winter,
Talked with them whene'er he met them,
Called them "Hiawatha's Chickens".

Of all beasts he learned the language,
Learned their names and all their secrets,
How the beavers built their lodges,
Where the squirrels hid their acorns,
How the reindeer ran so swiftly,
Why the rabbit was so timid,
Talked with them whene'er he met them,
Called them "Hiawatha's Brothers".

Henry Wadsworth Longfellow

47

THE EAGLE

He clasps the crag with crooked hands;
Close to the sun in lonely lands,
Ringed with the azure world, he stands.

The wrinkled sea beneath him crawls;
He watches from his mountain walls,
And like a thunderbolt he falls.

Alfred, Lord Tennyson

WHITE BUTTERFLIES

Fly, white butterflies, out to sea,
Frail, pale wings for the wind to try,
Small white wings that we scarce can see,
Fly!

Some fly light as a laugh of glee,
Some fly soft as a long, low sigh;
All to the haven where each would be,
Fly!

Algernon Charles Swinburne

THE WITCHES' SPELL *(Macbeth)*

Double, double, toil and trouble;
Fire burn, and cauldron bubble.
Fillet of a fenny snake
In the cauldron boil and bake;
Eye of newt, and toe of frog,
Wool of bat, and tongue of dog,
Adder's fork, and blind-worm's sting,
Lizard's leg and owlet's wing,
For a charm of powerful trouble,
Like a hell-broth, boil and bubble.
Double, double, toil and trouble;
Fire burn, and cauldron bubble.

William Shakespeare

THE TWELVE DAYS OF CHRISTMAS

On the twelfth day of Christmas
My true love sent to me
Twelve lords a-leaping,
Eleven ladies dancing,
Ten pipers piping,
Nine drummers drumming,
Eight maids a-milking,
Seven swans a-swimming,
Six geese a-laying,
Five gold rings,
Four colly birds,
Three French hens,
Two turtle-doves, and
A partridge in a pear-tree.

Anonymous

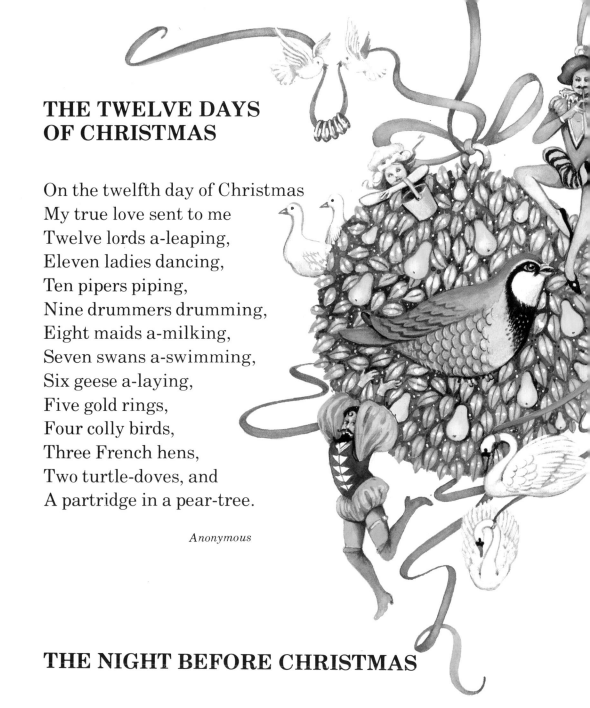

THE NIGHT BEFORE CHRISTMAS

'Twas the night before Christmas, when all through the house
Not a creature was stirring, not even a mouse;
The stockings were hung by the chimney with care,
In hopes that St. Nicholas soon would be there;

The children were nestled all snug in their beds,
While visions of sugar-plums danced in their heads;
And mamma in her 'kerchief, and I in my cap,
Had just settled our brains for a long winter's nap,
When out on the lawn there arose such a clatter,
I sprang from the bed to see what was the matter.
Away to the window I flew like a flash,
Tore open the shutters and threw up the sash.
The moon on the breast of the new-fallen snow
Gave the lustre of mid-day to objects below,
When, what to my wondering eyes should appear,
But a miniature sleigh, and eight tiny reindeer,
With a little old driver, so lively and quick,
I knew in a moment it must be St. Nick.
More rapid than eagles his coursers they came,
And he whistled, and shouted, and called them by name:
"Now, *Dasher!* now, *Dancer!* now, *Prancer* and *Vixen!*
On, *Comet!* on, *Cupid!* on, *Donder* and *Blitzen!*
To the top of the porch! to the top of the wall!
Now dash away! dash away! dash away all!"
As dry leaves that before the wild hurricane fly,
When they meet with an obstacle, mount to the sky,
So up to the house-top the coursers they flew,
With the sleigh full of toys, and St. Nicholas too.

And then, in a twinkling, I heard on the roof
The prancing and pawing of each little hoof.
As I drew in my head, and was turning around,
Down the chimney St. Nicholas came with a bound.
He was dressed all in fur, from his head to his foot,
And his clothes were all tarnished with ashes and soot;
A bundle of toys he had flung on his back,
And he looked like a peddler just opening his pack.
His eyes – how they twinkled! his dimples how merry!
His cheeks were like roses, his nose like a cherry!
His droll little mouth was drawn up like a bow,
And the beard of his chin was as white as the snow;
The stump of a pipe he held tight in his teeth,
And the smoke it encircled his head like a wreath;
He had a broad face and a little round belly,
That shook, when he laughed, like a bowlful of jelly.
He was chubby and plump, a right jolly old elf,
And I laughed when I saw him, in spite of myself;
A wink of his eye and a twist of his head,
Soon gave me to know I had nothing to dread;
He spoke not a word, but went straight to his work,
And filled all the stockings; then turned with a jerk,
And laying his finger aside of his nose,
And giving a nod, up the chimney he rose;
He sprang to his sleigh, to his team gave a whistle,
And away they all flew like the down of a thistle.
But I heard him exclaim, ere he drove out of sight,
"Happy Christmas to all, and to all a goodnight."

Clement C. Moore

QUEEN MAB

A little fairy comes at night,
Her eyes are blue, her hair is brown,
With silver spots upon her wings,
And from the moon she flutters down.

She has a little silver wand,
And when a good child goes to bed
She waves her hand from right to left,
And makes a circle round its head.

And then it dreams of pleasant things,
Of fountains filled with fairy fish,
And trees that bear delicious fruit,
And bow their branches at a wish:

Of arbours filled with dainty scents ·
From lovely flowers that never fade;
Bright flies that glitter in the sun,
And glow-worms shining in the shade:

And talking birds with gifted tongues,
For singing songs and telling tales,
And pretty dwarfs to show the way
Through fairy hills and fairy dales.

Thomas Hood

THE POBBLE WHO HAS NO TOES

The Pobble who has no toes,
Had once as many as we;
When they said, 'Some day you may lose them all';
He replied, 'Fish, fiddle-de-dee!'
And his Aunt Jobiska made him drink
Lavender water tinged with pink!
For she said, 'The World in general knows
There's nothing so good for a Pobble's toes!'

The Pobble who has no toes
Swam across the Bristol Channel;
But before he set out he wrapped his nose
In a piece of scarlet flannel.
For his Aunt Jobiska said, 'No harm
Can come to his toes if his nose is warm;
And it's perfectly known that a Pobble's toes
Are safe – provided he minds his nose!'

The Pobble swam fast and well
And when boats or ships came near him,
He tinkledy-binkledy-winkled a bell,
So that all the world could hear him.
And all the Sailors and Admirals cried
When they saw him nearing the further side –
'He has gone to fish for his Aunt Jobiska's
Runcible Cat with crimson whiskers!'

But before he touched the shore,
The shore of the Bristol Channel,
A sea-green Porpoise carried away
His wrapper of scarlet flannel.
And when he came to observe his feet,
Formerly garnished with toes so neat,
His face at once became forlorn,
On perceiving that all his toes were gone!

And nobody ever knew,
From that dark day to the present,
Whoso had taken the Pobble's toes,
In a manner so far from pleasant.
Whether the shrimps or crawfish grey
Or crafty Mermaids stole them away –
Nobody knew: and nobody knows
How the Pobble was robbed of his twice five toes!

The Pobble who has no toes
Was placed in a friendly Bark,
And they rowed him back, and carried him up
To his Aunt Jobiska's Park.
And she made him a feast at his earnest wish
Of eggs and buttercups fried with fish –
And she said – 'It's a fact the whole world knows
That Pobbles are happier without their toes!'

Edward Lear

RAIN

The rain is raining all around,
It falls on field and tree;
It rains on the umbrellas here,
And on the ships at sea.

Robert Louis Stevenson

HORSES OF THE SEA

The horses of the sea
Rear a foaming crest,
But the horses of the land
Serve us the best.

The horses of the land
Munch corn and clover,
While the foaming sea-horses
Toss and turn over.

Christina Rossetti

WHO HAS SEEN THE WIND?

Who has seen the wind?
Neither I nor you:
But when the leaves hang trembling
The wind is passing thro'.

Who has seen the wind?
Neither you nor I:
But when the trees bow down their heads
The wind is passing by.

Christina Rossetti

TIME TO RISE

A birdie with a yellow bill
Hopped upon my windowsill,
Cocked his shining eye and said:
"Ain't you 'shamed, you sleepy-head?"

Robert Louis Stevenson

57

MERRY AUTUMN DAYS

'Tis pleasant on a fine spring morn
To see the buds expand,
'Tis pleasant in the summertime
To see the fruitful land;
'Tis pleasant on a winter's night
To sit around the blaze,
But what are joys like these, my boys,
To merry autumn days!

We hail the merry autumn days,
When leaves are turning red;
Because they're far more beautiful
Than anyone has said.
We hail the merry harvest time,
The gayest of the year;
The time of rich and bounteous crops,
Rejoicing and good cheer.

Charles Dickens

THE KITTEN AND
THE FALLING LEAVES

See the kitten on the wall,
Sporting with the leaves that fall!
Withered leaves, one, two, and three,
From the lofty elder-tree.
Through the calm and frosty air
Of this morning bright and fair,
Eddying round and round they sink
Softly, slowly. One might think,
From the motions that are made,
Every little leaf conveyed
Some small fairy, hither tending,
To this lower world descending.
– But the kitten, how she starts!
Crouches, stretches, paws, and darts!
First at one, and then its fellow,
Just as light, and just as yellow.
There are many now – now one –
Now they stop and there are none.
What intentness of desire
In her upturned eye of fire!
With a tiger leap halfway,
Now she meets the coming prey.
Lets it go at last, and then
Has it in her power again.

William Wordsworth

A SONG ABOUT MYSELF

There was a naughty boy,
A naughty boy was he,
He would not stop at home,
He could not quiet be –
He took
In his knapsack
A book
Full of vowels
And a shirt
With some towels –
A slight cap
For a night-cap –
A hair brush,
Comb ditto,
New stockings,
For old ones
Would split O!
This knapsack
Tight at's back
He rivetted close
And followed his nose
To the North,
To the North,
And followed his nose
To the North.

There was a naughty boy,
And a naughty boy was he,
He ran away to Scotland
The people for to see –
There he found
That the ground
Was as hard,
That a yard
Was as long,
That a song
Was as merry,
That a cherry
Was as red,
That lead
Was as weighty,
That fourscore
Was as eighty,
That a door
Was as wooden
As in England –
So he stood in his shoes
And he wondered,
He wondered,
He stood in his shoes
And he wondered.

John Keats

TRAVELLING

One leg in front of the other,
One leg in front of the other,
As the little dog travelled
From London to Dover.
And when he came to a stile –
Jump! he went over.

Anonymous

WINTER

When icicles hang by the wall,
And Dick the shepherd blows his nail,
And Tom bears logs into the hall,
And milk comes frozen home in pail;
When blood is nipp'd and ways be foul,
Then nightly sings the staring owl,
To-whit! to-who!
A merry note,
While greasy Joan doth keel the pot.

When all aloud the wind doth blow,
And coughing drowns the parson's saw;
And birds sit brooding in the snow,
And Marian's nose looks red and raw;
When roasted crabs hiss in the bowl,
Then nightly sings the staring owl,
To-whit! to-who!
A merry note,
While greasy Joan doth keel the pot.

William Shakespeare

WINDY NIGHTS

Whenever the moon and stars are set,
Whenever the wind is high,
All night long in the dark and wet,
A man goes riding by.
Late in the night when the fires are out
Why does he gallop and gallop about?

DECEMBER

A wrinkled crabbed man they picture thee,
Old Winter, with a rugged beard as grey
As the long moss upon the apple-tree;
Blue-lipt, an ice drop at thy sharp blue nose,
Close muffled up, and on thy dreary way
Plodding along through sleet and drifting snows.
They should have drawn thee by thy high-heap't hearth,
Old Winter! seated in thy great armed chair;
Watching the children at their Christmas mirth;
Or circled by them as thy lips declare
Some merry jest, or tale of murder dire,
Or troubled spirit that disturbs the night;
Pausing at times to rouse the smouldering fire,
Or taste the old October brown and bright.

Robert Southey

Whenever the trees are crying aloud,
And ships are tossed at sea,
By, on the highway, low and loud,
By at the gallop goes he.
By at the gallop he goes, and then
By he comes back at the gallop again.

Robert Louis Stevenson

MY SHADOW

I have a little shadow that goes
    in and out with me,
And what can be the use of him
    is more than I can see.
He is very, very like me from
    the heels up to the head;
And I see him jump before me,
    when I jump into my bed.

The funniest thing about him
    is the way he likes to grow—
Not at all like proper children,
    which is always very slow;
For he sometimes shoots up taller
    like an India-rubber ball,
And he sometimes gets so little
    that there's none of him at all.

He hasn't got a notion of how
    children ought to play,
And can only make a fool of me
    in every sort of way.
He stays so close beside me,
    he's a coward you can see;
I'd think shame to stick to nursie
    as that shadow sticks to me!

One morning very early,
    before the sun was up,
I rose and found the shining dew
    on every buttercup;
But my lazy little shadow,
    like an arrant sleepy-head,
Had stayed at home behind me
    and was fast asleep in bed.

Robert Louis Stevenson

WHAT IS PINK?

What is pink? A rose is pink
By a fountain's brink.

What is red? A poppy's red
In its barley bed.

What is blue? The sky is blue
Where the clouds float through.

What is white? A swan is white
Sailing in the light.

What is yellow? Pears are yellow,
Rich and ripe and mellow.

What is green? The grass is green,
With small flowers between.

What is violet? Clouds are violet
In the summer twilight.

What is orange? Why, an orange,
Just an orange!

 *Christina Rossetti*

THE DAFFODILS

I wandered lonely as a cloud
That floats on high o'er vales and hills,
When all at once I saw a crowd –
A host of golden daffodils
Beside the lake, beneath the trees,
Fluttering and dancing in the breeze.

Continuous as the stars that shine
And twinkle on the Milky Way,
They stretched in never-ending line
Along the margin of a bay:
Ten thousand saw I, at a glance,
Tossing their heads in sprightly dance.

The waves beside them danced, but they
Out-did the sparkling waves in glee:
A poet could not but be gay,
In such a jocund company:
I gazed – and gazed – but little thought
What wealth the show to me had brought:

For oft, when on my couch I lie
In vacant or in pensive mood,
They flash upon that inward eye
Which is the bliss of solitude;
And then my heart with pleasure fills,
And dances with the daffodils.

William Wordsworth

PIPPA'S SONG

The year's at the spring,
And day's at the morn;
Morning's at seven;
The hill-side's dew-pearled;
The lark's on the wing;
The snail's on the thorn;
God's in His heaven –
All's right with the world!

Robert Browning

UPON THE SNAIL

She goes but softly, but she goeth sure;
She stumbles not as stronger creatures do:
Her journey's shorter, so she may endure
Better than they which do much further go.

She makes no noise, but stilly seizeth on
The flower or herb appointed for her food,
The which she quietly doth feed upon,
While others range, and gare,* but find no good.

And though she doth but very softly go,
However 'tis not fast, nor slow, but sure;
And certainly they that do travel so,
The prize they do aim at, they do procure.

*Gare: stare about.

John Bunyan

67

THE VILLAGE BLACKSMITH

Under a spreading chestnut-tree
The village smithy stands;
The smith, a mighty man is he,
With large and sinewy hands;
And the muscles of his brawny arms
Are strong as iron bands.

His hair is crisp, and black, and long,
His face is like the tan;
His brow is wet with honest sweat,
He earns whate'er he can,
And looks the whole world in the face,
For he owes not any man.

Week in, week out, from morn till night,
You can hear his bellows blow;
You can hear him swing his heavy sledge,
With measured beat and slow,
Like a sexton ringing the village bell,
When the evening sun is low.

Henry Wadsworth Longfellow

TREES

The oak is called the king of trees;
The aspen quivers in the breeze;
The poplar grows up straight and tall;
The pear tree spreads along the wall;
The sycamore gives pleasant shade;
The willow droops in watery glade;
The fir tree useful timber gives;
The beech amid the forest lives.

Sara Coleridge

WHEN THE COWS COME HOME

When the cows come home
   the milk is coming,
Honey's made while the bees
   are humming;
Duck and drake on the rushy lake,
And the deer live safe
   in the breezy brake;
And timid, funny, brisk little bunny
Winks his nose and sits all sunny.

Christina Rossetti

OLD MEG

Old Meg she was a Gipsey,
And liv'd upon the Moors;
Her bed it was the brown heath turf,
And her house was out of doors.

Her apples were swart blackberries,
Her currants, pods o'broom;
Her wine was dew of the wild white rose,
Her book a churchyard tomb.

Her Brothers were the craggy hills,
Her Sisters larchen trees;
Alone with her great family
She liv'd as she did please.

No breakfast had she many a morn,
No dinner many a noon,
And, 'stead of supper, she would stare
Full hard against the moon.

But every morn, of woodbine fresh
She made her garlanding,
And, every night, the dark glen Yew
She wove, and she would sing.

And with her fingers, old and brown,
She plaited Mats o' Rushes,
And gave them to the cottagers
She met among the Bushes.

Old Meg was brave as Margaret Queen
And tall as Amazon;
An old red blanket cloak she wore,
A chip hat had she on.
God rest her aged bones somewhere!
She died full long agone!

John Keats

THE LADY OF SHALOTT

On either side the river lie
Long fields of barley and of rye,
That clothe the wold and meet the sky;
And through the field the road runs by
To many-towered Camelot;
And up and down the people go,
Gazing where the lilies blow
Round an island there below,
The island of Shalott.

Willows whiten, aspens quiver,
Little breezes dusk and shiver
Through the wave that runs for ever
By the island in the river
Flowing down to Camelot.
Four grey walls, and four grey towers,
Overlook a space of flowers,
And the silent isle imbowers
The Lady of Shalott.

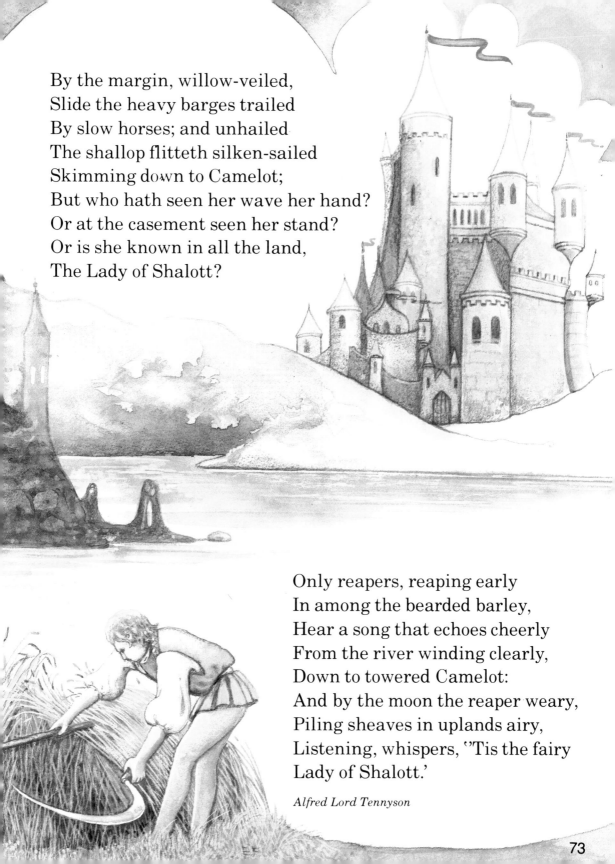

By the margin, willow-veiled,
Slide the heavy barges trailed
By slow horses; and unhailed
The shallop flitteth silken-sailed
Skimming down to Camelot;
But who hath seen her wave her hand?
Or at the casement seen her stand?
Or is she known in all the land,
The Lady of Shalott?

Only reapers, reaping early
In among the bearded barley,
Hear a song that echoes cheerly
From the river winding clearly,
Down to towered Camelot:
And by the moon the reaper weary,
Piling sheaves in uplands airy,
Listening, whispers, ''Tis the fairy
Lady of Shalott.'

Alfred Lord Tennyson

MINNIE AND WINNIE

Minnie and Winnie
Slept in a shell.
Sleep, little ladies!
And they slept well.

Pink was the shell within,
Silver without;
Sounds of the great sea
Wandered about.

Sleep, little ladies!
Wake not soon!
Echo on echo
Dies to the moon.

Two bright stars
Peeped into the shell.
"What are they dreaming of?
Who can tell?"

Started a green linnet
Out of the croft;
Wake, little ladies!
The sun is aloft.

Alfred, Lord Tennyson

THE OWL

When cats run home and light is come,
And dew is cold upon the ground,
And the far-off stream is dumb,
And the whirring sail goes round,
And the whirring sail goes round;
Alone and warming his five wits,
The white owl in the belfry sits.

When merry milkmaids click the latch,
And rarely smells the new-mown hay,
And the cock hath sung beneath the thatch
Twice or thrice his roundelay,
Twice or thrice his roundelay;
Alone and warming his five wits,
The white owl in the belfry sits.

Alfred, Lord Tennyson

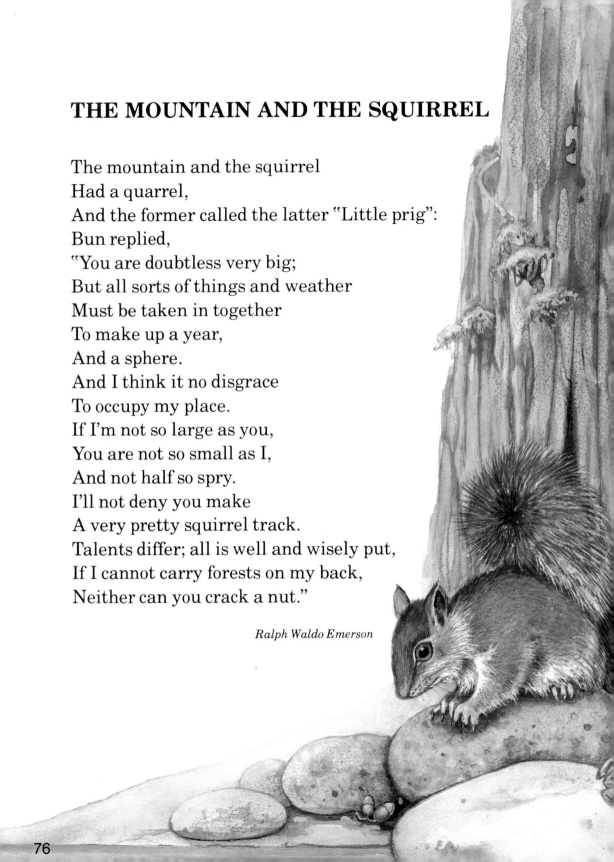

THE MOUNTAIN AND THE SQUIRREL

The mountain and the squirrel
Had a quarrel,
And the former called the latter "Little prig":
Bun replied,
"You are doubtless very big;
But all sorts of things and weather
Must be taken in together
To make up a year,
And a sphere.
And I think it no disgrace
To occupy my place.
If I'm not so large as you,
You are not so small as I,
And not half so spry.
I'll not deny you make
A very pretty squirrel track.
Talents differ; all is well and wisely put,
If I cannot carry forests on my back,
Neither can you crack a nut."

Ralph Waldo Emerson

BE LIKE THE BIRD

Be like the bird, who
Halting in his flight
On limb too slight
Feels it give way beneath him,
Yet sings,
Knowing he hath wings.

Victor Hugo

THE FAIRIES

Up the airy mountain,
Down the rushy glen,
We daren't go a-hunting,
For fear of little men.
Wee folk, good folk,
Trooping all together;
Green jacket, red cap,
And white owl's feather!

Down along the rocky shore
Some make their home.
They live on crispy pancakes
Of yellow tide-foam;
Some in the reeds
Of the black mountain lake,
With frogs for their watchdogs,
All night awake.

William Allingham